NEW JERSEY
portrait of a state

NEW JERSEY
portrait of a state

GRAPHIC ARTS BOOKS

The following photographers hold copyright to their images as indicated:
Howard Ande, page 31; Jon Arnold/DanitaDelimont.com, pages 30, 85, 98;
Bill Bachmann/DanitaDelimont.com, page 32; Scott Barrow, pages 1, 13, 14, 17, 28–29,
47, 68, 79, 86, 104, 108–9; Cut and Deal, Ltd./IndexOpen.com, page 24; Tim Fitzharris,
pages 46, 48, 67, 76a, 76b, 76c, 76d, 89; Steve Greer, pages 2, 6, 7, 8–9, 9, 10, 11a, 11b, 25, 26,
27a, 27b, 27c, 33, 35, 36, 37, 39, 43, 52, 54, 65, 70, 71, 74, 75, 77, 81, 82, 83, 84, 94, 102, 103, 106;
J. J. Raia, front and back cover, pages 4–5, 16, 18, 19, 20, 22, 23, 34, 38, 40, 41, 42, 44–45, 49, 50,
51, 53, 55, 56–57, 58, 59, 60, 61, 62, 63, 64, 66, 69, 72–73, 78, 92, 95, 96, 99, 100–101, 105, 107,
110, 111, 112; James J. Stachecki, pages 12, 15, 21, 29, 80, 87, 88–89, 90, 91, 93, 97.

Library of Congress Control Number: 2007929886
International Standard Book Number: 978-0-88240-695-4

Captions and book compilation © 2007 by
Graphic Arts Books, an imprint of
Graphic Arts Center Publishing Company
P.O. Box 10306, Portland, Oregon 97296-0306
503/226-2402; www.gacpc.com

The five-dot logo is a registered trademark of
Graphic Arts Center Publishing Company.

President: Charles M. Hopkins
Associate Publisher: Douglas A. Pfeiffer
Editorial Staff: Timothy W. Frew, Kathy Howard, Jean Bond-Slaughter
Production Coordinators: Heather Doornink, Vicki Knapton
Cover Design: Elizabeth Watson
Interior Design: Jean Andrews

Printed in the United States of America

FRONT COVER: ❡ Point Pleasant Beach was spotted
on September 2, 1609, by Henry Hudson and the crew of his
ship, *Half Moon*, on their way north to explore the Hudson River.
BACK COVER: ❡ Cheesequake State Park includes open fields, saltwater and
freshwater marshes, a white cedar swamp, Pine Barrens, and a northeastern hardwood forest.
◀◀ The Delaware Water Gap includes some forty miles of the middle Delaware River and
almost seventy thousand acres of land along the river's New Jersey and Pennsylvania shores.
◀ At sunset, a starfish adorns the sandy beach at Sea Bright, on the New Jersey shore.
▶ Cherry blossoms add delicate color at Branch Brook Park, in Newark. Branch
Brook is the first county park in the United States to be opened to the public.

◄ Autumn leaves brighten the Batsto River,
in Wharton State Forest. The state forest is the largest
single tract of land protected by New Jersey's state park system.
▲ Fall cranberry harvest is in full sway in Chatsworth. It is believed that
cranberries were first cultivated in New Jersey in 1840 by John Webb.
He sold them to merchant ships for $50 a barrel. With their
high vitamin C content, they helped ward off scurvy.

◄ The tidal salt marsh of the Great
Bay Wildlife Management Area, shown here
at high tide, is a great place for canoeing or kayaking.
▲ A Pine Barrens male tree frog sings in Pinelands
National Reserve, which is classified as a
United States Biosphere Reserve.

9

◄ A Christmas Day reenactment of George Washington
crossing the Delaware Bay depicts the crossing in daylight. The actual
crossing, in 1776, took place in the dead of night during a blinding snowstorm.
▲ TOP TO BOTTOM: ◗ An actor plays the part of Dr. Emlen Physick in the library
of the Emlen Physick Estate (constructed from 1879 to 1881) in Cape May.
◗ Victorian ladies enjoy Afternoon Tea at the Mainstay Inn, built
as an exclusive clubhouse in 1872 in Cape May.

▲ The iridescent green head identifies a mallard drake
in Dover's Hedden Park. The mallard *(Anas platyrhynchos)*
is probably the best known of all ducks.

▲ The annual Beach Patrol Competition in
Monmouth County includes swimming in strong
currents, running on soft sand, rowing, paddling, and
kayaking through a shoulder-high beach break, and saving
"victims." The Monmouth team usually manages
to stay near the top of the competition.

▲ A Sussex County farm is blanketed in snow.
▶ A tufted titmouse *(Parus bicolor)* rests on a snow-
covered branch with holly berries near Dover. The bird's
range has moved farther north in recent years, possibly
as a result of more people having bird feeders.

◄ The Wyanokie Mini-Circular Trail heads into
Norvin Green State Forest. Many popular hiking trails
in the area were blazed by the Green Mountain Club in the 1920s.
▲ A small waterfall graces Schooley's Mountain County Park.
The park offers numerous recreational opportunities,
such as fishing, bridle trails, boating, and ice skating.

▲ Brightly hued flowers carpet a meadow in Somerset County.
▶ Hanks Pond is just one of the jewels of the Pequannock Watershed.
Only forty miles from New York City, the watershed offers thirty-
five thousand acres of unspoiled, peaceful wilderness.

◄ Bullfrog Pond is situated in Lord
Stirling Park, part of the Great Swamp near
Basking Ridge. A variety of wildlife inhabits the area.
▲ A beehive in Hedden Park, Dover, helps
to keep the ecosystem healthy.

21

▲ Morning fog hovers over marsh
grasses in Wildwood Crest, in Cape May.
The first house in Wildwood Crest was built in 1906.
▶ Wild wisteria blooms in a small open space in Edison.
Edison, a town of more than one hundred thousand
residents, was named the twenty-eighth most
livable small city in America in 2006.

◄ With the shore, the Boardwalk, colorful
nightlife—even a burger stand and Trump's
Taj Mahal—Atlantic City has something for everyone.
▲ A naturalist and students have fun along with the serious
business of planting beach grass at Island Beach State Park.

▲ The Peaslee Wildlife Management Area provides
opportunity to explore a pitch pine forest. Peaslee encompasses
three main habitats: Atlantic white cedar swamps,
pitch pine lowland, and hardwood swamps.

▲ CLOCKWISE FROM TOP LEFT: Though highly
populated by humans, wildlife still abounds in New Jersey—
● A red fox *(Vulpes vulpes)* hunts for prey in the snow at Island Beach State Park.
● A white-tailed deer *(Odocoileus virginianus)* interrupts her grazing to care for her fawn.
● A North American beaver *(Castor canadensis)* cuts down a large oak tree.

◄ The Passaic River, a tributary
of Newark Bay, flows out of the 7,600-
acre Great Swamp National Wildlife Refuge.
▲ A green heron *(Butorides virescens)* waits for prey
on a stump in the Great Swamp. The green heron is one
of the few tool-using birds. It commonly drops bait
onto the surface of the water and snatches
the small fish that are lured.

◄ Victorian houses line a street in Cape May.
▲ The Port J train of Metro-North arrives at a station
in Jersey City. The New Jersey Transit is under contract to
supervise operation of the Metro-North trains
west of the Hudson River.

▲ The New York Giants played their first game
in Giants Stadium on October 10, 1976, against the
Dallas Cowboys. The stadium is actually located in New
Jersey, just under seven miles from Times Square.

▲ A young girl gets a popcorn treat
at the Moorestown Hardware store. In
2005, Moorestown was named the best place
to live in America by *Money* magazine.

▲ Sea Bright Beach is known for
its private beach clubs and restaurants.
▶ A path wends its way through the
coastal sand dunes in Avalon.

34

◄ American white water lilies
bloom in a pond along Dividing Creek
in Cumberland County in southern New Jersey.
▲ A horse farm radiates peace. Rural activities include
hayrides, corn mazes, farm stands, school tours, agricultural
fairs, farm festivals, winery tours, and horseback riding.

▲ Maples in autumn brighten Ramapo Mountain Reservation.
▶ In Wharton State Forest in the Pine Barrens, fire both destroys
and renews. Some plant species die off, at least temporarily,
in a burned-over area; others need fire to open up the
canopy overhead so they get more sun.

◄ Makepeace Lake Wildlife
Management Area, situated in the heart
of Atlantic County in Hamilton Township,
encompasses more than ten thousand acres.
▲ Saint Lucia brightens Atlantic County.

▲ Twenty-eight-hundred-acre Supawna Meadows National
Wildlife Refuge is a part of the Cape May National Wildlife Refuge.
▶ A delicate orchid shade tints mountain laurel in the Pine Barrens.
▶▶ At dawn, the South Seaside Park horizon seems on fire.

◄ A pileated woodpecker *(Dryocopus pileatus)* pokes its head
out of a nest hole. Nearly as large as a crow, the pileated woodpecker
digs for ants in trees. Their excavations can actually break small trees in two.
▲ The Sandy Hook Lighthouse was constructed in 1764 to protect ships. Today
it is the nation's oldest lighthouse still in use. Sandy Hook became the site of
Fort Hancock, an important part of the nation's coastal defense until 1974.

▲ A northern saw-whet owl looks out
on the world from a frame of rosehips. The
northern saw-whet *(Aegolius acadicus)* is a small owl,
averaging only seven to eight inches long.

▲ Sumac, shown here in Morris
County, turns a brilliant crimson in autumn.
There are some 250 species of sumac, including several
poisonous varieties: poison ivy, poison oak, and poison sumac.
Morris County is located in north-central New Jersey.

▲ A birch stand highlights Liberty State
Park. Formally opened on Flag Day, June 14, 1976,
as New Jersey's bicentennial gift to the nation, Liberty
State Park is situated less than two thousand
feet from the Statue of Liberty.

▲ Now enshrouded in ice, Spruce Run
State Park is enjoyed by picnickers, swimmers,
fishermen, boaters, campers, and hikers
when weather is a bit milder.

▲ Amusement rides are a
part of the experience at Ocean City.
▶ The shores of Steenykill Lake, in High Point
State Park, abound in color. Dedicated in 1923,
High Point was New Jersey's first state park.

◄ Blazing star blossoms carpet a meadow in
Hunterdon County, in the west-central part of the state.

▲ Swamp mallow *(Hibiscus moscheutos)* graces Spruce Run
State Park. Swamp mallow is also called rose mallow.

►► Blue Mountain Lakes dot the Delaware Water
Gap National Recreation Area.

◄ North Wildwood Beach presents a vista
much like those seen by the Lenni Lenape Indians, who
visited the area for pleasure and relaxation in the early 1600s.
▲ Marsh mallow blossoms brighten Meadowlands Marsh. Marsh mallow
is just one of some one thousand varieties of mallow, many
of which are used for food and medicine.

▲ Beech leaves add color to the Ken Lockwood
Gorge, in the New Jersey Highlands. The South Branch of
the Raritan River tumbles through the gorge, splashing over
numerous rocks into rapids, small waterfalls, and pools.
▶ Autumn grasses and blueberries create a collage of
brilliant color in Pinelands National Reserve.

◄ A young white birch stand flourishes
in the Delaware Water Gap National Recreation Area.
▲ The Makepeace Wildlife Management Area is administered
by the New Jersey Division of Fish and Wildlife.

▲ The six-hundred-acre Spruce Run Recreation
Area, with 1,290 acres of water, offers summertime
swimming, fishing, boating, picnicking, and camping.
▶ Massive icicles formed onto a limestone overhang
at Dunnfield Creek in Worthington State Forest.

65

◄ Speedwell Lake, in Morris County, covers about twenty
surface acres, providing great boating and fishing opportunities.
▲ Both male and female eastern bluebirds have an orange-tinted
throat, but the male's is a brighter orange, and his blue
back and tail are a brighter blue than the female's.

▲ The historic Red Mill, rising beside
the Raritan River in Clinton, New Jersey, is now
home to the Hunterdon Historical Museum. The Red Mill
was constructed as a gristmill in 1812 to process wool.
▶ A small brook gurgles over rocks in
Spruce Run State Park.

◄ A fast-flowing river continues to shape the Delaware Water Gap.

▲ Some ten miles of coastal dunes on Island Beach remain almost untouched
since Henry Hudson first saw the New Jersey coast from his ship, the *Half Moon*, in 1609.

►► Among other attractions, Wawayanda State Park features an Atlantic white cedar
swamp, a mixed oak-hardwood forest, and a spring-fed lake.

◄ Cape May has a fascinating history—and is also a place
that offers much contemporary action. Among the amenities
are an active marina with slips available as well as boat rentals.
▲ Green Sergeant's Covered Bridge, situated near Flemington in
Hunterdon County, was constructed in 1750. It is the
only covered bridge remaining in New Jersey.

▲ CLOCKWISE FROM TOP LEFT: Wildlife in New Jersey includes—
 ● An American mink *(Mustela vison)*, once heavily hunted for its fur;
 ● A bobcat kitten *(Lynx rufus)*, native to North America, but seldom seen;
 ● A long-eared owl *(Asio otus)*, similar in appearance to great horned owls;
 ● A porcupine *(Erethizon dorsatum)*, whose range covers much of North America.
 ► A baby opossum *(Didelphis virginiana)* hangs from a branch in Pine Barrens.
 The opossum is the only North American marsupial (female with a pouch).

◄ Manasquan was settled by Europeans in
1685, when the owners of the Manasquan Beach
Company bought the area from American Indians. Still a
popular getaway, the dunes retain much of their original beauty.
▲ This section of the Delaware and Raritan Canal is situated near Stockton,
in Huntingdon County. Some thirty-six miles of the main canal still exist.

▲ Alpacas graze at Brookhollow Farm, in Boonton Township.
▶ A foggy sunrise at the Palmyra Nature Cove Park reveals part of a 350-acre
island of green in a highly developed area along the Delaware River.

◄ Mount Tammany reaches an elevation of 1,527 feet.
▲ Batsto Village, located in Wharton State Forest, was founded in
1766 by Charles Reed, who constructed the Batsto Iron Works on the banks
of the Batsto River. When the pig iron industry waned in the mid-1800s, the area
turned for a time to glassmaking, then to cranberry production. Now the
centerpiece of the Wharton State Forest, it is maintained as a
historical site as well as for the beauty of the area.

▲ A painter leans out a window to paint
Kirby's Mill in Medford. It is believed that the area was
inhabited as long as four thousand years ago.

▲ On Cape May, a Victorian house is
part of an unparalleled collection of Victorian
houses. Cape May also holds the distinction of being
the oldest seashore resort in the United States.

▲ Bay Head, on the Jersey Shore, maintains
a casual decor along with the elegance nature supplies.
▶ Parrot tulips are cultivated in Parsippany, paying tribute
to New Jersey's nickname of the "garden state."

◄ Tivoli Gardens is a center of peace in
Parsippany. *Parsippany* comes from the Lenape word
for "the place where the river winds through the valley."
▲ The curved front claws and powerful hind legs make
the red squirrel *(Tamiasciurus hudsonicus)*
a very good climber and jumper.

◄ Buttermilk Falls cascades some eighty to ninety
feet down the face of the Kittatinny Ridge, near Branchville.
▲ Fall color in Sussex County shows a variety of colors
ranging from greens to yellows to reds.

▲ Wild mustard flourishes beneath a tree in Troy Meadows.
When the last glacier retreated from what is now called New Jersey,
part of it broke off and sat where the Troy Meadows are now, forming
a big bowl. The present Troy Meadows have remained a swamp.
▶ Although swans generally mate for life, they do occasionally
"divorce," especially if a nesting failure has occurred.

◄ A snow-covered farmhouse in
Mount Laurel creates a Christmas-card image.
▲ In winter, a young maple raises its leafless branches in the
Delaware Water Gap National Recreation Area.

▲ Spring buds bring hope of new life in Lewis
Morris Park. Named for New Jersey's first governor,
the park opened in 1958. Since that time the county park
has grown from 350 acres to over a thousand acres.

▲ A trunk and leaves create
an interesting pattern in a stand of
birch trees. With its white trunk, the birch
has been known as "the white tree."

▲ Barnegat Light, commissioned January 1, 1859, was built to
replace the original light, put in service in 1835. The present Barnegat
Light was decommissioned in January 1944 and is now open to the public.
▶ Sawmill and Marcia lakes are sister lakes in High Point State Park. Sawmill
Lake offers overnight accommodations; Marcia is restricted to day use only.
▶▶ Fog shrouds the river at Delaware Water Gap National Recreation Area.

◄ Young raccoons explore their
new world in New Jersey's Pine Barrens.
▲ A great horned owl *(Bubo virginianus)* takes flight
in Medford. A very large owl, the great horned owl ranges
from eighteen to twenty-seven inches long, with a
wingspan of from forty to sixty inches.

▲ The Great Hall on Ellis Island was opened
to the public after renovation was completed in 1990.
Although Ellis Island is in New Jersey waters, it is governed by
New York. It served as a door for immigration from 1892 to 1943
and was used for immigrant detention until 1954. In 1965, it
became part of the Statue of Liberty National Monument.

▲ Daylilies and crown vetch mix in Hunterdon County.
Daylilies are not true lilies, but their name does indicate an
interesting point: each individual flower lasts only one day, to
be replaced by a new blossom the next day. Crown vetch is also not
a true vetch, though it closely resembles the common vetch.

▲ Tufted vetch brightens a meadow in the Peaslee
Wildlife Management Area. At twenty-five thousand acres,
Peaslee is New Jersey's second-largest wildlife management area.
▶ At sunrise, Atlantic City takes on an otherworldly look.
▶▶ The Milford Bridge crosses over the Delaware
River between Milford, New Jersey, and
Upper Black Eddy, Pennsylvania.

▲ Vine maples embellish 2,145-acre
Ramapo Mountain Reservation in autumn.
► Magnolia petals add color to Holmdel Arboretum.
►► An autumn cascade breaks the flow of
Middle Brook in Somerset County.